Stop and Look

by Gemma Ridgway-Faye

Stop and look in the park or garden.
What can you see?

The morning is bright and fresh. Blink and scan the garden.

There is a nest in the treetop.
It is a thrush.

This one is slim and black. It has spun a web from stem to stem.

Look in the shallow pond. A frog swims. It jumps.

Is that a track on the bank? Is that a skid in the mud?

This crow drags a big stick.

It flaps up into the air.

A skink is in the sun. It is hot on the step.
brown skin

There is a bee. It hovers near a flower.

Look at this. The smell is sweet.
I bend down to sniff it.

It is dark at night. Look up. It is a thrill!

Quick, there is a tail. It looks like a brush.

A possum can swing with its tail.

A bat hangs in the starlight.

It clings to the trunk up high.

Stop and look. What can you see in the park or garden?

Look Back

Encourage students to use the images to review the topic.